I0415490

The Conservative Liberal Legitimacy Game

Political Polarization and Division over Historical Perception in Korea

Seong Jun Park

ISBN: 1491203579
ISBN-13: 978-1491203576

DEDICATION

To the People of Bugil Academy

CONTENTS

Acknowledgments   i

1   Introduction   1

2   The Conservative World View: 3

3   The Conservative Approach to Solving Problems   9

4   The Conservative Exhibition of Doctrines   20

5   One History, Two Perceptions: Syngman Rhee and the ROK   26

6   One History, Two Perceptions: Chung Hee Park and His 18 Years   36

7   Impact of Political Disposition on Historical Perceptions   51

8   Conclusion   59

9   Works Cited   61

10   About the Author   66

ACKNOWLEDGMENTS

I would like to express my gratitude to many people who saw me through this book; to all those who provided support, talked things over, read, wrote, offered comments, allowed me to quote their remarks and assisted in the editing, proofreading and design.

I would like to thank my Directed Research Project instructor Dr. Rebecca Kuhn who guided me through this writing and spent her valuable time in reading and commenting my long and tedious paper despite her busy schedule. Without her guidance, this publication would never have been possible.

I would also like to thank my mentor Mr. Graham Wik and advisor Mr. Christopher DeCou for encouraging and counseling me.

Thanks to my English instructor Mr. Steve Feldman whose strictness when grading my essays forbade me from lowering my guard against wordiness.

Not to forget Mr. Joong Kwon Hahn who allowed me to interview him on one hot summer day in spite of my notoriety as a conservative.

Last and not the least, I beg forgiveness of all those who have been with me over the course of the years and whose names I have failed to mention.

Introduction

"History is nothing but a pack of tricks that we play upon the dead", said the French philosopher Voltaire (Durant). Indeed, the academic branch of history is a field in which thinkers from different sides mostly fight over interpretations rather than excavate the truth, if the truth is even possible. When history is closed in a politically-sensitive geographical interval, thinkers may be divergent and finding truth even more chaotic. Modern Korean historians perceive events differently depending on their political affiliations: Conservative or Liberal. The aim of this project is to analyze previous studies to understand the current characteristics of the conservative group in Korea, their general perceptions and beliefs, and how they differ from those of reactionaries and liberals. How conservatives and liberals' political dispositions differentiate their perception of history and how they use this difference of perception to reinforce their political legitimacy is the central backbone of this research.

Korean conservatives, while they are not successors of classical conservatives in western society, are epistemologically similar to them based on the four pillars: perception of the world as a single body, anti-utopianism, absence of concrete idealized objectives and distrust of human rationality. These pillars make conservatives to value institutions, power and, limiting freedom and equality and thus lead them to evaluate President Rhee and Park positively as figures who embodied these principles for nation-building. Korean liberals are epistemologically opposite from the four pillars and oppose institutions and power while promoting equality. This leads them to evaluate the two presidents negatively as dictators whose actions cannot be justified.

The Conservative Worldview

It is essential to understand conservatism's epistemological nature in order to apprehend how conservatives perceive history different from liberals. A clear distinction should be made between conservatives and reactionaries. Often, the two political groups are confused as being identical; even politicians mix the terms without much caution. Lee Jung Hee, a former Presidential candidate for the United Progressive Party (UPP) stated in her speech accepting Presidential candidacy, "While the reactionaries (referring to the conservative New Frontier Party) will try to alienate the liberal union through means of Red Scare and abuse of authority, we will fight on" (Lee, "UPP elects Lee and Shim"). The confusion in terminology results mainly from the fact that both conservatism and reactionary share certain characteristics. The two groups are similar in that both have disbelief towards human rationality and skepticism about democracy (N. Lee). However, conservatives differ from reactionaries in more ways.

The following sections will unravel the epistemological nature of conservatives that they exhibit a worldview based on four main platforms: the existence of the world as a single body, an anti-utopia view of the world, the absence of idealistic objectives and distrust of human rationality. It will also look at how the worldview of liberals and reactionaries are different from these four pillars.

World as a Single Body

Fundamentally, conservatives see the world as a single body. Their perception denies any other world other than the world that they currently reside in, and leads conservatives to treat any non-conforming social element as an abnormality that disturbs the unity of that single world. This is a characteristic that distinguishes reactionaries from conservatives. Reactionaries perceive the world as a body of two separated spaces, the current world and an older world. To reactionaries, the possibility of a different world spurs them to pursue an older world. Orthodoxy values the ancient and classical worlds as more valuable than the current world on ethical grounds, as they were untouched by the moral dilemma of the modern era (N. Lee).

It is highly interesting, even ironic that reactionaries and liberals share many similarities under this category (N. Lee). Liberals, like reactionaries, see the world as sets of different bodies. But the bifurcation that they see is the one between the status quo and the future.

Anti-Utopian

This bifurcated world view inevitably disposes reactionaries to be proponents of utopia, the possibility of an idealistic world. Conservatives, on the other hand, have no ideal world to pursue as the only metaphysical space real to them is the world in which they exist at the present moment. In other words, conservatives are anti-utopian, a characteristic that serves as the second pillar of their worldview. Conservatives acknowledge and recognize that problems exist under status quo and embrace those problems as part of the social world they live in.

Liberals embrace the possibility of utopia. However, unlike reactionaries, liberals do not look up to the past, but rather a future based on liberal values. Past is even detested as an immature stage of social development.

Absence of Concrete Idealistic Objectives

Because conservatives are anti-utopia, they seem to lack concrete, idealistic objectives; this is the third basic pillar of conservatism. Conservatives often do not have a specific, immediate purpose in acting and if there is one drive that directs conservatives to act, it is to continue the status quo. As mentioned above, conservatism arises directly from the sense that one belongs to a pre-existing social order. The continuation of the existing social order, represented through heritage and history, is the most important consideration for conservatives when making decisions. History, institutions and culture are viewed as the repositories of human values and are ends as well as means. For conservatives, having a society determine its purpose and objectives is irrational, needless and inefficient, for it destroys the fundamental relationship upon which society is based and order maintained. As Scruton argues, communism seems particularly absurd to conservatives since communism sees society entirely as a means to a future goal. To be true to their philosophical core, communists must therefore be at war with the very people they set out to govern (Scruton).

In accordance with this utopia, liberals have concrete idealized objectives. These idealized objectives have been the inspiration for revolutionary changes.

Distrust of Human Rationality

The last fundamental pillar of the conservative worldview is the irrationality of human minds. This pillar is much more epistemological than the previous pillars and in some respect, can be considered as the backbone of conservatism. Conservatives claim that men are incapable of controlling the shifts that occurs in the process of reorganizing social structure (N. Lee). Burke, displaying his great distrust of human rationality, said that "feeble materials easily walk the wrong path". American philosopher McCloskey based her summary of conservatism on Burke as well as those from Hernshow and Kirk. Her summary holds that conservatives believe that 1) obligation is much greater than rights; 2) the world is too complicated to apprehend unless one is an expert; 3) we cannot change our human instincts; 4) humans continuously become weak as they are grown with excessive playing on another's affection; 5) the heart and the brain are equal in terms of leadership; 6) while we should teach children that all men are created equal, some are superior to others; 7) business is carried out by a small number of distinguished men; 8) in the long run, only a few know what is best for him or herself (S. Yang). Most of the items in her summary are aiming at showing the limitations of human mindset.

Perhaps the most significant divergence between liberals and conservatives is their trust in human rationality. Liberals believe that people possess nearly unlimited capacity and therefore, there are no restraints on the use of the human mind (Scruton). To conservatives' distrust of human rationality, Nami Lee emphatically states that "Buddha sees Buddha and pigs see pigs; accordingly, if some men- conservatives- see others as those who'll incinerate society, they are actually the ones who ought to be chained up". She argues that conservatives embrace skepticism because they themselves are not competent enough to be confident of human potential. Liberals see that this capability of mankind is, as Thomas Jefferson would have said, "self-evident" since people design and construct ideal objectives.

The Conservative Approach to Solving Problems

The description of conservative characteristics explained above informs the conservatives approach to solving social problems. Muller demonstrates that a belief in human imperfection and epistemological modesty are keys to understand the conservative psyche. Viereck argues that conservatism uses the Christian principle that men are sinful to inform their approach to public policies. Muller goes further, saying that while assumption of a sinful nature may be grounded in religion, it can also be argued on secular grounds (Muller). He presents the argument developed by Arnold Gehlen that men are limited by their biological instincts for survival and the world is too complex for limited men to be able to solve problems alone. Hence, conservatives believe that they should call on guidance from a higher power, usually institutions.

Institutions

As mentioned earlier, conservatives see the world as one, indivisible spatial body, a social organism that does not have a utopian counterpart and is too complex to be understood or completely managed by mankind whose rationality is far too restricted. Thus, the optimum method to deal with the flawed world is to avoid seriously deforming the status quo. When the world and societies exist in their organic form, conservatism's four pillars are easily qualified. The emphasis on preserving social organization makes any change gradual and careful. For conservatives, society should not be subject to radical construction or destruction as heritage, history and tradition need to be preserved as they are the repositories of human-societal values that consistently interact to form the societal organism.

In society, men voluntarily merge with other men to create bigger groups to govern. More than any other animal, man is dependent upon other members of his species, and hence upon social institutions for guidance and direction (Muller). Institutions help people control their impulses and give constraints. Without constraints, conservatives fear that society will be deprived of this indispensable institutional element that would allow it to flourish. Institutions are needed to guide human passions appropriately and complement our limited human rationality. In *Reflections on the Revolution in France*, Burke demonstrated that "the restraints on men, as well as their liberties, are to be reckoned among their rights." For conservatives, institutions must be defended as they serve useful functions for society. Considerable changes to institutions may reduce the benefits they can offer to society, and at worst place society in chaos. Military, education, religion and traditional marriages are some of the greatest examples that conservatives would want to protect under this notion.

Liberals argue that conservatives overall are afraid of mass tyranny and want to check the people through institutions, as conservatives lack confidence in human nature. Liberals, in contrast to conservatives, see democratic ideals as ends. Liberals therefore embrace pure democracy as they believe that ultimate ends of society must not be oppressed.

The Need and Uses of Power

Since one of the main concerns of conservatism is maintaining institutions, conservative politics is concerned with "sustaining the life of [this institutional] organism, through sickness and health, change and decay" (Scruton) and are in conflict with the diseased and destructive factions of society. Modern conservative politicians see themselves as imperfect, like all other members of the human race, but they are responsible for healing the illness. They should not act as engineers who hastily disintegrate structures in order to build new ones. Conservatives seek to support society through authority which strengthens the existing institutional systems. The feeling of acceptance, manifest in patriotism, custom, respect for law, loyalty to a leader or monarch, or the willing acceptance of privileges from those to whom privilege is granted, can extend itself indefinitely (Scruton). From this feeling, the conservative politician derives his or her authority. It is crucial to remember that conservatives lack immediate purpose as mentioned earlier. Without immediate objectives, conservatives may seem to be blindly pursuing authority which makes them look Machiavellian. For conservatives, power is not subordinate to some clear justifying aim – it is not the means to social justice, or equality, or freedom (Scruton). Power exists to keep order through influence and command.

Limiting Freedom

Because reinforcing existing institutions and their authority is the primary focus of conservatism, conservatives are skeptical of those who challenge institutions and existing power structures. To repeat, for conservatives institutions are important and should be venerated so that they can accomplish future tasks. Anything that disturbs institutional focus is considered an abnormality. Democracy is often included in this category. The person who first coined the term "conservatism" was Edmund Burke who wrote in opposition to the French Revolution, an event he saw as destroying civilization. Conservatism is rooted in skepticism towards revolutions and their democratic goals (N. Lee). Scruton explains what freedom means to [British] conservatives. Freedom is not a precondition, but rather the result of accepted societal arrangements and order. Personal liberties are the outcome of the long social evolution of stable institutions. Thus, freedom without institutions is meaningless. Constraints on freedom are needed for freedom to exist at all. This is a major line that differentiates conservatives' look on freedom from the liberal look on freedom to exist at all. While to liberals, freedom is the absolute aim, to conservatives, freedom is subordinate to institutional authority.

Limiting Equality: Defending Elitism

Because the conservative affinity for authority and order and their distrust of human rationality, they tend to exhibit strong elitism (N. Lee). Conservatives believe that elites are required to stand against revolutionaries and those who practice civil disobedience. Elites should take on a greater burden than others in preserving knowledge and the arts, directing the commons, regulating organizations and keeping tradition for posterity. John Quincy Adams believed that the aristocracy was required to protect liberty from both King and the public and that claiming oneself to be a noble did not mean that he was ordained by blood, but means that he was a member of a natural elitist society within humanity (Viereck). Conservatives see the public as uncontrollable and unable to achieve institutional stability. Schumpeter argues that "even if there were no political groups trying to influence him, the typical citizen would in political matters tend to yield to extra-rational or irrational prejudice and impulse." Conservatives are skeptical of equality and social justice; they regard universal political agitation with distaste (Scruton). These demands only seem to threaten the political order.

Conservatives propose that the flaw of equality as an absolute value is that it does not occur in nature. This idea has been advocated by conservative theorists for centuries and is strengthened when related to efficiency and talent. W. H. Mallock, observing 19th century Industrial Britain concluded that material progress was based on unequal distribution and leadership from talented elites who use their abilities for economic advancement (Muller). Arguing based on Humean doctrine that economies should not and do not reward virtues, he stressed in *Aristocracy and Evolution: A Study of the Rights, the Origin, and Social Functions of the Wealthier Classes*, "the majority in any progressive community may not look forward to indefinitely better conditions, but merely that their condition will not depend on themselves, and that though the conditions of all may be bettered, they will never be even approximately equal" (Muller).

This support for elitist society serves as a basis for a political structure that puts a check on democracy. James Madison, in his Federalist Paper No. 10, argued for limiting "pure democracy" as it "can admit no cure for the mischief of faction". Madison argues that common passion or interest will be felt by a majority, and there is nothing to check the inducements to sacrifice the weaker party. Hence it is, that democracies have ever been found incompatible with personal security or the rights of property; and have, in general, been as short in their lives as they have been violent in their deaths (Bailyn). Hence, Madison echoes along the lines of John Stuart Mill's *On Liberty* and states that the "tyranny of the mass" can often be more formidable than political oppression by small group of individuals. Mill himself wrote that "when society is itself the tyrant, its means of tyrannizing are not restricted to the acts which it may do by the hands of political functionaries". This is exactly why many of the Founding Fathers of the United States-many of whom were members of the social elite whose espoused virtuous motivations were debatably weaker than their monetary motivations- were hesitant to grant everyone the same political power. They were aware of the fact that the newly independent persons of America could be tyrants themselves without the presence of "the tyrant" King George.

Even if most individuals could prove themselves rational, conservatives would still disagree with democracy because of their Critique of Theory. Liberals and radicals are said to depend upon a systematic, deductivist, universalistic form of reasoning. For conservatives, this reasoning fails to account for the complexity and peculiarity of the institutions the liberals and radicals seek to reform (Muller). It is true that liberals have been successful at vocalizing and organizing their ideological aims in a theoretical manner. Again, conservatism historically developed as a response against liberalism and lacking a clear-cut objective, they tend to keep themselves away from formularizing their beliefs into written principles and actively vocalizing them. However, this doesn't mean that they are opposed to logical theorization entirely. What conservatives oppose are epistemologically haughty forms of knowledge and analysis (Quinton). They believe that when liberals simplify nature they lack the care which enables people to comprehend the complexity of social institutions. Burke demonstrated that approaches to societal, democratic virtues are ought to be case-specific as they "vary with times and circumstances and admit to infinite modifications... and cannot be settled upon any abstract rule". Conservatives fear that theorization may cause them to act under one mindset for the betterment of institutions and ignore the fact that we should not expect the same consequences for every case.

Today, democracy is a popular government form that conservatives have had to adapt. Defending their position of skepticism towards democratic theories and knowing that there is a serious discrepancy between theory and democratic practice in reality they have tried to redefine the concept of democracy as not to be direct rule by the people, but as a governance by a selected group of people. Under this definition, democracy means "only that the people have the opportunity of accepting or refusing the men who are to rule them" (Schumpeter). Schumpeter goes further to describe the ideal government as one that employs "the services of a well-trained bureaucracy of good standing and tradition, endowed with a strong sense of duty and a no less strong *esprit de* corps". Conservatives feel that emphasis on direct input from the masses is hazardous as the purpose of representative democracy is giving power to the representative so that he or she can craft the best public policy.

In addition to favoring pure democracy, liberals reject Mallock's idea that inequality is natural and effective. Conservatives' phobia towards the irrational selfishness of the mass is non-existent in the liberal mindset. The Russian evolutionary scientist and liberal philosopher Peter Alexeyevich Kropotkin stressed that people are more capable of cooperating than competing in his critique of the capitalist system. In his work *Mutual Aid: A Factor of Evolution*, he stated "The animal species, in which individual struggle has been reduced to its narrowest limits, and the practice of mutual aid has attained the greatest development, are invariably the most numerous" (Kropotkin). Although he acknowledged some benefits of competition, he perceived competition as destroying more goodness than it builds. This view that is shared by many liberals has led them to emphasize cooperation in specific policies such as taxation. Whereas increasing progressive taxes is an unfair measure against rightful competition and individual accomplishment in the eyes of conservatives, it is a virtuous collective sacrifice in the eyes of liberals.

The Conservative Exhibition of Doctrines

The epistemological factors that underpin conservatism as well as the conservative approach to solving social problems make hard to clarify conservatives' historical interpretations since they base their observations of history not only on their natural inclination, but also specific political doctrine that arise from the epistemological underpinnings. These doctrines are statism, nationalism and libertarianism.

Statism

Statism, initially, is a belief that the government should have control over the economy, social policy, or both. With the importance of institutions in the conservative mindset already established, it is easy to understand why conservatives believe that the state should influence these areas. However, as will later be discussed, this contradicts conservatives' libertarian views and will be addressed later on.

Nationalism

Nationalism, the second platform, is much more significant in that it is an overarching theme in histories of almost all nations and is getting more attention in the academic world since the early 1990s. In the recent revisionist history movement, nationalism has been considered as a mechanism that conservatives have used to stabilize their authority. For example, the case of post-1848 Europe, the conservative governments in Austro-Hungarian and the German Empire, led by Bismarck, were able to consolidate their status and quell resistance by using nationalism to bring the major classes together under one objective (Greene). By promising to gradually expand suffrage and political benefits to the citizenry, conservative leaders appealed to the liberal middle class and socialist working class who demanded political participation and improvement in their economic conditions. The conservatives ensured that the nation's advancement by correlating the two promises together. They urged all classes to devote themselves to nation-building, which the other two classes willingly agreed to in return for economic prosperity. In Japan, after the

Meiji Restoration, conservatives appealed to the nation through a similar strategy and the public responded vigorously. Japan was able to make notable military achievements and bring wealth into the country.

Not surprisingly, liberals respond with skepticism and objections towards statism. In the Korean context, interestingly, liberals are proponents of nationalism. However, their nationalism is used to call upon the union of Korean liberals to oppose conservatives and the conservative government whose relationship with the United States is intimate. Liberal thinkers argue that Pro-American, foreign-reliant conservatives are betraying Korea's nationalist principles. Liberals oppose statism and its institutional authority.

Libertarianism

Scruton stresses that true conservatism is not intrinsically connected to the market economy and capitalism. However, it is dangerous to argue that economic libertarianism is irrelevant and denounce it as a sudden creation of Reagan or Thatcher when it is a common theme that is articulated by conservatives in most, if not all nations.

As mentioned above, conservatives are elitist and, in more traditional terms, aristocratic by nature. Just as

Schumpeter proposes that elites make compromises with pure democracy, conservatives understand that aristocracy cannot be sustained as civil society develops. Conservatives still believe and argue that an aristocratic spirit should be preserved. However, the structure of most liberal democracies forbids the creation of a specific, designated class for leadership. Hence, conservatives advocate a social structure which bases itself on individual ability and accomplishment; a social structure made most possible by advocating for a free market economy and capitalism (N. Lee). Support for individual superiority is a variation on support for class superiority.

In *Thoughts and Details on Scarcity,* Burke argued for limiting the state from intervening in private matters because a system based on private property is the cornerstone of societal formation. Conservatives therefore focus on preserving the free market economy which appreciates the freedom of capitalist society and the creativity of private enterprise. Conservatism tends to turn to libertarian thoughts to explain itself (Viereck). Modern conservatives thus desire to interpret classical conservatism in a libertarian, rationalist way, and this is parallel to the tendency which colonialism and imperialism become similar to libertarianism if made more moderate (N. Lee). There is a value in doing so, according to an American sociologist Robert Nisbet. He argues that the reason why conservatism is connected to libertarianism is because of libertarianism's rational aspects justifies conservatism; libertarianism is between the extremes of left and right; and libertarianism aims to improve conservatism's social acceptability (Nisbet).

Liberals despise libertarianism more than statism, as liberals value economic equality over economic competition. The two concepts cannot coexist (Nisbet). Nami Lee enthusiastically criticizes libertarianism, saying that Hobbes's philosophy that the fear having life, liberty and property taken away dehumanizes humankind. There can be no desire to protect the weak in a world obsessed with competition and freedom to achieve success. This is why liberals support a strong welfare state. Korea, uniquely, is undergoing an unbelievable upsurge of demand for utopian welfare state programs. Since 2010, there have been consistent voices for nationwide free cafeterias in schools and half-price college tuition. If the first demand were fulfilled, more urgent and necessary spending would have been sacrified. However, destabilizing the treasury, liberals nevertheless continued to demand this policy (Choi, "Collapse of the Nation by Making Cafeteria Free").

Seong Jun Park

One History, Two Perceptions: Syngman Rhee and the ROK

Historians' main job is to assess and evaluate what has already happened. They may be more biased than other intellectuals in such sense and in Korea where thirty-five years of Japanese colonial rule has left the nation with historical severance the degree of polarization is more extreme than in other areas of the world (Cummings). When these biased intellectuals collide, it is usually conservatives responding to a liberal interpretation as conservatives have the lighter task of writing the history of the victor – conservatives have been in control of the government since 1948 except from 1997 to 2007.

The Identity of Rhee's Presidency and
the Republic of Korea

The most interesting yet bewildering fact about the political and historical controversy surrounding Korea is that the legitimacy of the state and its government is frequently questioned, challenged, denied and in response, heatedly defended by its own citizens. When examining political cleavages and disputes over historical interpretations, it is rare that a direct debate over the notion of the state itself occurs. The controversies tend to revolve around specific elements of the state, usually figures and particular policies. For example, many British may hate Thatcher and what her government did but would not abominate the United Kingdom for the laws enacted under its name. However, many Koreans do deviate from this trend. While acknowledging the legitimacy of the state, they initiate fights about Korea's national identity (Cho). In 2012 alone, when media began to report on "Neo-Communist Infiltration", at least two newly-elected members of parliament refused to pledge allegiance to the flag or sing the national anthem, claiming that such rituals were unjust simple mechanisms of the state to cover up its flawed past of hindering the freedom and justice it stands for on paper (Yang, "Lee Seok Gi refuses Aeguka").

The central figure of this controversy is Syngman Rhee (1875~1965), the first President of the Republic of Korea. As one of the late Chosun reformists who argued for a groundbreaking structural reform of the country into a western model, he lived most of his early years in exile in the United States, organizing independence movements there during the Japanese colonial era. After returning to Korea following independence in 1945, he was supported by the United States and notable Korean dignitaries to establish the Republic of Korea in 1948 and become its first President. He is known to have proposed the division of the country in order to keep capitalism in the south and to have passed two constitutional amendments to extend his presidency. Finally in 1960, a nationwide revolution toppled his government and he died in exile in 1965.

The Conservative Judgments on Rhee's Presidency

The conservative side of perceiving the founding of the Republic in 1948 is a story of rightfulness and pioneering. Conservatives view that while the autonomy and independence of the peninsula was limited, the founding faction of the country made the best decision under such constrained conditions.

Conservatives assert that while it is true that ROK did not receive full support from the public and had extensive cooperation with foreign powers, it was a legitimate government that optimized its stability in the midst of the Cold War. Conservative historians contend that while Rhee was never truly pro-American, he considered America to be an incredible ally. Based on his compilation and analyses of the Department of State documents between 1919 and 1955, Yeong Ik Yoo explains Rhee acknowledged that the U.S. could abandon the new Korean Republic just as it abandoned the Korean Empire. Throughout the Korean War, Rhee consistently maneuvered his forces separately from the UN command and in order to guarantee his government's status, freed anti-communist North Korean POWs thereby sending a message to the West that without proper guarantees his government would act without their consent or opinion. Yoo argues that the Mutual Defense Treaty between the United States and Korea was the epitome of "Rhee's sharp comprehension of international politics which his liberal counterparts lacked". Rhee succeeded in consolidating the U.S.'s aid and post-war protection that shielded the recovering nation from harm.

In terms of founding-fatherhood, conservatives state that Rhee and his colleagues delineated ROK's direction that precipitated the nation's course of advancement. Despite much of the criticism of the Rhee government for unilaterally oppressing the left and blocking other parties from influencing the ROK during the post-independence period, conservatives argue that these actions enabled the establishment of the Republic and thus, its Constitutional democracy and free economy. Conservatives often compare the post-independence leaders of Korea and India: Rhee and Jawaharlal Nehru. The prevailing idea from this comparison is that while Rhee's method may have been partially problematic and arbitrary at the end of his term, his design for a new nation was much more stable and well-guided than that of Nehru. Jihyang Park, professor at Seoul National University asserts that Rhee's outline for the new Korean nation was undeniably a success when contrasted with that of India and especially when the state of the two countries are placed parallel to each other. He states that while Nehru was libertarian to the degree of calling himself the "last British over India", his political disposition was also influenced by socialism that he had adopted in his youth. Hence, he promoted political democracy and accommodated a Soviet-style controlled economy, suppressing the private economic sector. Park arges that Nehru left India burdened with economic backwardness along with Gandhi's anti-industrial, village-centered economy. Rhee, on the other hand, made a decisive decision to select democracy and capitalism as the system of the new Republic.

To conservatives, Rhee is an ideal model of who solidified a sound basis for the institution that is most essential to the conservative psyche. To them, Rhee's flexibility was a key to the nation's survival, his Machiavellian tug-of-war with powers around him being an example of how an authority should work for the preservation of his institution.

The Liberal Judgments on the Presidency of Rhee

Before discussing this dispute any further, one phenomenon that must be identified is that Korean liberals are highly critical of the ROK. While they might not be as extreme as the two MPs who refused the pledge and the anthem, most of them question whether the nation was established adequately under proper people. Joong Kwon Hahn, the head of a liberal organization True-Education League in Gyeongnam

Province explains this liberal skepticism by pointing out that the ROK was a creation of opportunistic, foreign-dependant conservatives without any liberal input, arguing that the conservatives repeated the same used an outer, foreign power in 1948 and relied on America to consolidate their privileges. He argues that a similar even occurred when the ruling conservatives of Silla relied on Tang China to unify the peninsula and that both Goryeo and Chosun relied on Chinese hegemony to suppress domestic turbulence. Hahn points to the fact that the ROK's founding faction were right-wing collaborators, who had endorsed and worked for the Japanese under colonial rule and who later cooperated the same with the temporary U.S. military government (1945~1948). Cummings presents an identical image of the conservative faction of the time noting that they "lacked nationalist credentials". He even claims that "the United States intervened on behalf of the smallest group, the privileged right-wing in Korea and helped to perpetuate its privileges thereafter" and that "had the Americans quit Korea, a leftist regime would have taken over quickly, and it would have been a revolutionary nationalist government, that, over time, would have moderated and rejoined the world community- as did

China, as Vietnam is doing today".

In Cummings proposal of an ideal left-wing government under the presumption of the U.S.'s vacancy, a notable tendency closely connected to the liberals' challenges of the ROK's identity emerges- a sympathetic attitude for the legitimacy of North Korea. It may be astounding to see Korean citizens actually sympathizing with the country's worst enemy, but after 1945 the only alternative to the right-wing were communists, it seems that the liberals take North Korea as the antithesis of the ROK that they question when they evaluate history. Liberals' viewpoint of left-right conflicts shortly after independence and the Korean War highlights the liberals' relative affinity to North Korea as a liberal alternative to the ROK.

A stark difference between Korean conservatives and liberals can be seen on how they discuss the 4.3 Jeju incident and YeoSun incident. Liberals view that it was less of an attempted rebellion to capsize the government, but more of an unavoidable outburst by frustrated liberals who demanded land redistribution without compensation to landlords, a purge of police and other officials who had served under the Japanese and the suspension of establishing a separate government in the

South. By denying any possibility of Pyeongyang's influence over the incidents, Cummings and Hahn justify the rebellion and temporary anarchy in Jeju, Yeosu and Suncheon as natural civil movements while harshly criticizing the ROK's brutal quelling "directed by Americans and carried out by young Korean colonels" (Cummings). Both Cummings and Hahn claim that these incidents underline ROK's exploitive and oppressive characteristics and that it was founded against the will of the masses. With respect to the Korean War, Cummings extends his claim of America's puppet play by saying that the reason for ROK's early losses in the war was because it was being commanded under racist, misunderstanding Americans and hypocritical Korean elites who had collaborated with the Japanese. In contrast, he portrays North Korea to have been "never simply a Soviet satellite, but [an entity] evolved from a coalition regime based on widespread people's committees", thereby emphasizing the "majority's will" in establishing the DPRK in opposition to ROK's elitist, suppressive and foreign-reliant nature. Hahn even goes further and states that Kim Il Sung had more legitimacy than Rhee as Kim actually led a tangible guerrilla against the Japanese while Rhee was often ignored by his fellow nationalist colleagues due to his subservience to Washington. In summary, liberals consider that the characteristics of the founding faction of the ROK led to "the country's initial structural problem that has induced Korea's social paradoxes" (Choi) such as social inequality, polarization and foreign-reliance.

Seong Jun Park

One History, Two Perceptions: Chung Hee Park and His 18 Years

Chung Hee Park came to power in 1961 through military coup in which he promised the nation to resolve political instability after Rhee's resignation. He also promised to return to his role as soldier after this goal is met but never kept this promise, being elected as President for three consecutive terms. In 1972, he enacted the Yushin Constitution that gave him the control of all three governmental branches and quelled the opposition. He was eventually assassinated by his head of intelligence in 1979. As the president with the longest term in office in Korean history, Park is criticized for his dictatorship and militarization of the nation. He is at the same time, praised and revered for his charismatic leadership in spurring Korea's industrialization.

The Conservative Judgments on the Presidency of Chung Hee Park

Chung Hee Park is an absolute icon in Korean conservatism who many conservatives respect as Korea's "Best President". Those who do not go as far as to call him the best consider him the optimum leader of his time. Their argument is fairly simple as conservatives tend to avoid structuralizing their doctrines and their historical interpretation mostly arise in order to react to that of liberals. The defense of Park's legacy began in the early 1990s when the leftist revisionist school of history reached its peak following Cummings's success in leading young intellectuals against the traditional school. Conservatives felt the risk of having their most basic values and accomplishments jaded as liberals began to interpret their era of nation-building as an "era of suppression of the mass-led reforms" or a "period of capitalist feudalism" (Cummings).

Conservatives propose that Park and his governance was the only option that Korea could choose at the time and that while there may have been components that are unsatisfactory considering the standards of substantive democracy, it saved the fate of the country forever. Conservatives suggest that Park saw reality: it was impossible for Korea impossibility to break its congested semi-feudal society in a process similar to that of Europe two centuries earlier. Korea was two centuries behind and the only method to abridge this gap was groundbreaking reforms. The limitations of a soft state inherited from the previous dynastical order, in which the central authority was only mighty on the surface, required a nationwide change. Korea's modern day achievements were the products of the "nation-building generation" who modernized the country by repressing fundamental rights and some democratic values (Cho).

Liberal critics argue that economic development could and should have happened without dictatorship. Conservatives respond with the definition of poverty stated by Amartya Sen (though ironically some of Sen's ideas are against conservatism) that it is "the lack of freedom to have or to do things that you value". To conservatives, since poverty is not merely low income or absence of abundance, but a state without any concrete capability for future improvement, asserting that the situation would have been better without Park's style of development is a frustrating hindsight bias. Conservatives are irritated by liberal historians who are, by conservative standards, "reversing the beginning and the end" (Cho). They assert that while a civil regime after the April Revolution of 1960 may have attempted to achieve similar success, the lack of a charismatic leader like Park would have prevented the growth of both economy and maturity of democracy. After all, it is important to note that democracy and civil society grew along with or after the formation of a stable middle class that could mediate the age of transition (Viereck). Conservatives rhetorically ask whether Korean society is able to embrace both the excess and deficiency of Park's leadership and hence to look at modern history with a wider, accepting perspective. Thus, they applaud to the works of sociologist Taejun Kwon, who renounced his leftist stand. He said, "The market itself cannot be the mechanism of accumulating wealth. Was this country was left alone, would it have overcome the traditional congestions and have evolved into a progressive political system? This assumption has subconsciously seeped into our criticisms of authoritarian industrialization. Repeating, it is a stretched assumption that free democracy would have spontaneously molded the high living standards of today" (Kwon). Thus, conservatives express their skepticism towards democracy and propose that it would not have been an effective alternative for Park's government.

As conservatives defend Rhee as having set Korea on the path of successful nation-building, they uphold Park as a figure who detailed this blueprint and put it into reality. Conservatives, whom many of them are the members of the older nation-building generation, remember the 60s and the 70s with nostalgic admiration for a strong, determined leadership and Park's personal image of self-sacrifice- which liberals condemn as propaganda- adds even greater element of veneration. Certainly, Park relied on nationalism, urging the public to devote themselves to nation-building, and provided the nation that he promised to his supporters. Conservatives view his authoritarian system to have been a reasonable and unavoidable tradeoff. While it may have caused lasting problems as well, it gave the succeeding generations the leisure of thinking about such social problems. To conservatives, Park was the apex of what conservatives uphold. He promoted statism, nationalism and libertarianism and skillfully interpreted them to strengthen his authority and the institution.

The Liberal Judgments on the Presidency of Chung Hee Park

Chung Hee Park is a non-excludable figure who determined the fate of the country until now. After coming to power through military coup in 1961, he served as President for 18 years and even attempted to consolidate his life-long term through a highly resented constitutional amendment until his assassination in 1979. Liberals view his presidency as the source of lasting problems in Korea in terms of central authoritarianism and centralism, parochialism and division, social inequality and class polarization, and foreign-reliance.

i) Central Authoritarianism

The major criticism that Park and his regime face from liberals is that it was authoritarian, centralizing everything to the President himself. Conservatives and liberals agree that Park was a dictator and used suppressive methods in maintaining his power for 18 years. Liberals however place much stricter, even harsher standards on Park when evaluating his era. They specifically target Park's nullification of the constitutional order, containment of civil society and bureaucratization of the government.

Overall, Korean liberals tend to refuse to recognize Park as a proper, legitimate President on the reason that Park nullified and destroyed the constitutional order and thereby disrupted the most fundamental principle of democracy on which he claimed to rule. Jae Hong Kim argues that "abnormalities dominated the Park's era especially in the political structure" and points out that the ruling political parties were poli-technologically structured entities, meaning that they were not formed under spontaneous groupings of politically homogeneous persons. The President's henchmen technically manipulated the parties and the democratic system was never a substantive one. Kim presents the 10.2 Crisis, in which the failure of the ruling party in 1971 to pass a Park-sponsored resolution due to internal strife led the Korea Central Intelligence Agency (KCIA) to arrest and torture the "problematic" MPs and force them to resign, an equivalent to a gang punishing an internal traitor.

Park's control over politics reached its epitome with the declaration of the Yushin Constitution –named after the Meiji Restoration to signify revolutionary change– which permitted the suspension of all freedom and rights if necessary and paved the way for Park's eternal reign.

Civil society faced its greatest challenge. Liberals claim that Park's reign was worse than that of the Japanese occupation (Kim). According to Kim, the control over media was conducted differently from the colonial censorship which censored the contents of what was published. Park went further, controlling the press itself and thus containing any chance of civil voice affecting his office. Even more drastic was his attempt to control the mindset of the public, liberals say. Park was the biggest beneficiary of the Cold War and he used this situation to mold the ideology of the day (Cummings). Korea was a "Garrison State" in that the entire country was forced to serve as a huge military unit prepared with permanent anxiety to react to communist threat (Kim). Any expression related to anti-government or pro-leftist movements were banned and could be used to convict anyone for treason. It was required that the Korean citizenry think in only one way; education was used to raise youth under a military fashion. Inadvertently, civil expression as a whole had to be checked. Liberals see Park as the source of stiffened Korean civil culture even to this day. Society had to ignore the protests of the labor force and those who thought differently causing tension in the country (J. Choi). This was because Park didn't see the mass as a group to cherish and look after, but as a resource group to mobilize (Kim).

Even excluding Park himself, liberals say that Park's regime itself was intolerant, elitist and therefore exclusive of the masses. Former American diplomat to Korea Gregory Henderson also discusses the severe bureaucratization that resulted from the absence of civil society and centralization of power during the Park era. He refers to Tocqueville's theory on the development of the imperious French bureaucracy as a byproduct of the French Revolution that decimated the suitable middle group, the feudal nobility. He then compares this case with the situation of Korea. Choi adds that the state bureaucracy was strengthened to the point that the public's relationship to politics was limited and the central elite more isolated (J. Choi). Choi concludes that with the absence of civil society, the overpowered and over-centralized bureaucracy monopolized every social resource and hindered competition between elites themselves. This over-simplified the structure of government and reinforced the authority-driven elitist foundation that enabled the state to oppress the masses even more with greater force.

ii) **Parochialism and Division**

Liberals perceive that the intrinsic top-down nature of bureaucracy and the existence of a single absolute figure leading the government led to the extreme geographic centralism that Korea faces today. They argue that while power was being centered under Park's stringent bureaucratic system, the regime was purposely dividing the nation. Henderson asserts that "Seoul was not just Korea's largest town; it was Korea". Liberals argue that political centralization also caused economic, social and cultural centralization towards the capital which created an overlapping of these various types of centralizations, forming a concentric structure (J. Choi). This centralization kept elites from considering wider issues outside of the centre and developed their desire to monopolize power, rather than integrating and cooperating with others. The best way to ensure this monopoly was to form a secure support group that would sustain their power with full, unchanging fidelity. Today region-based politics and parties competing with the support of their respective loyal regions dominate the country's politics which is still characterized with the division between the conservative east Yeongnam region and the liberal west Honam region. This divided up the nation already divided up into Seoul and the provinces and this split arguably helped the authoritarian regime in preventing the national mass from forming a union against it.

iii) Social Inequality and Class Polarization

The most appealing liberal argument in the current recession-struck society is the social inequality argument. The liberal side of the story of economic development under Park is a story of class struggle between the privileged, industrialized business conglomerates, also known as Chaebeols, and the unprivileged working class. It is also a story of imbalanced development and favoritism.

Park's economic development was an odd combination of mercantilist governmental control and capitalism that aimed for maximum outcomes, mostly from exports (Schuman). The Korean economy indebted with credit to foreign states ever since independence, quickly realized that exports were the solution to resolve financial difficulties. The government again employed military style of economic planning with itself serving as the "general HQ to command enterprises, its sub-regiments, storm foreign markets" (Schuman). It also established KOTRA (Korea Trade-Investment

Promotion Agency) to "cover" this pioneering move while constantly spurring businesses to meet the set objectives.

The crux of the liberal criticism lies in this style of development that had the government and businesses, especially Chaebeols, working as a single body, with the government offering something more than just help. From 1961, all exported items received complete tax exemptions and exporting companies were granted special loans at which the government offered an outstanding 6% interest rate compared to 25% in the market. In 1972, when companies could no longer withstand the debt they accumulated to build their size, the government even froze all business transactions in the country to save them.

This extraordinary favoritism is where liberals consider social inequality to have originated facilitated by modern day corruption and unequal treatment. Liberals see that the privileged group arose from placing all the burden of social cost on the socially unprivileged majority (J. Choi). The administration failed to achieve minimal equity and abandoned its responsibility to lessen this gap. Socially, this wrongful structure of "the survival of the fittest", "winner take all" that seeped into modern Korean mentality developed into an expedient trend that can be observed in all sectors of the nation. Consequently, the majority that could not access these expediencies could not improve their conditions and the wider gap exacerbated class polarization. As mentioned earlier, because the regime saw the public as a resource subject to mobilization, its genuine intention of industrialization was never on the advancement of the people's needs, but on fulfilling the demand of its clients, the privileged (Kim). In other words, liberals believe that Park's economic development was for his own political stability, not for the entire nation as Hahn argues.

iv)   Foreign-Reliance

Lastly, the extended continuation of criticisms on Rhee's foreign-reliance takes its place among liberals' thoughts on Park. Park's success in developing the economy is another field of debate for liberals. Some contend it was Park's remarkable achievement while others argue that it was simply the result of luck and situational advantages formed by foreign influence. Liberals think that Park inevitably would have seen the economy advance due to an influx of credit and foreign support. Hahn asserts that it was impossible for Park to fail to industrialize given the resources Park had at his disposal and if Park did fail, it would have only proved his incapacity even more. This claim was materialized into "The Hundred Years War", a highly controversial film made by the Institution for Research in Collaborationist Activities, a leftist organization, in the spring of 2013. Under the overarching theme of how Korea's privileged minority represented through Rhee and Park ineffectively controlled the country for a century with foreign endorsements, the film presents an argument through the Fraser Report, an investigation record on Koreagate incident published by Congress, that Park never envisioned export-led industrialization, but simply followed Washington's decision to aid and direct Korea's economy in order to contain communism. From there, the film goes further to claim that Park never decided anything on his own but relied heavily on this extended Korean version of the Marshal Plan. In other words, just as the film quotes from the Fraser Report, "[America] tutored Park the basics of governance". This film then relates Park's relationship with the U.S. to Korea's servility with the U.S., stating that Korea's economic independence was reduced to a puppetry performance and Park as served nothing more than a U.S.-sponsored dictator.

Park's relationship with Japan is even more controversial due to his personal history of serving in the Imperial Japanese Army before independence. Hahn, Choi and Kim criticize the reestablishment of diplomatic relations with Japan in 1965 as revealing Park's identity as a former collaborator. Liberals point out that Park renounced Korea's anspruch for Japan's colonial rule for credits and see his attitude towards Japan as "full of indignity" (Cummings). They state that 1965 set the tone of unequal relations with Japan which still causes trouble until today (J. Choi).

Impact of Political Disposition on Historical Perception

The incursion into epistemological foundations of conservatives and liberals contribute to how they interpret modern history in such way and why they cling so strongly on to them.

Cherishing the Moment

Some people may find it hard to understand conservatives' pride that they have towards modern history in spite of how the 20th century opened tragically for the Korean nation. However, it is the crux of conservatism to embrace the status quo regardless of whether society is entrenched with flaws or not. With no intent to wage war against the status quo, conservatives leave the solution to social problems up to gradual societal development. With this faith that good administration will advantage society, conservatives focus on institutional governance. This is why conservatives appreciate Rhee and Park's "efficient" government that incorporated all three components of conservative methods of solving problems: statism and nationalism.

If democratic value is the ultimate barometer in deciding which group gets the power, conservatives are undeniably in an unfavorable position in Korea as they wear the bridle of the autocratic past that liberals have crowned them with. Yet, it is important to remember that conservatism as a philosophy was never based on such values changing society to fit in the first place, but on properly and conservatively maintaining the status quo and checking radicalism, as discussed earlier. Conservatives would risk portraying a Machiavellian image for adequate governance as the two Presidents did. Conservatives see little problem with Rhee and Park as they believe that firm institutional stability is a prerequisite for a sound society, arrived after the necessary economic conditions were provided.

Conservatives further evaluate Rhee and Park highly on the basis that though they attained firmness in the Republic of Korea, Korean nationhood, this firmness could only be preserved with additional adjustments to the changing globe. In one phrase, the conservative side of modern Korean history is a story of success and it is a trophy that proves the conservative cause.

The stark difference between conservatives and liberals is that fundamentally conservatives are not strangled to a chain of doctrines and thus enjoy relatively greater freedom in politics. Furthermore, as they focus on preserving society through institutions, they are arguably more successful in efficient management than liberals who focus more on concrete ideologies. This practicality approach worked in the 2012 election as Park got elected despite earlier predictions that Moon who lost by a substantial margin with his grand liberal coalition would either match or exceed Park's votes. The main reason for liberals' defeat was the different historical approaches that were projected during their campaigns. While Moon concentrated on degrading Park and her father's autocratic faults and led his slogan of "protecting democracy from dictator's revival", Park confronted these criticisms and admitted her father's wrongs but confined her apologies to a statement that the decisions of her father were "unavoidable by the situation". The voters were first confused by Moon's somewhat outdated slogan of democracy, given that democracy itself was erected in 1987. To them, Park's promises to reconstruct the very positive glories of Park's era were more appealing and voters chose practical management over ideological game. Another possible reason was that Moon appeared far too radical and Park seemed to be a better insurer of the Miracle of the Han River already given that negative sentiments towards Jung Hee Park was much smaller than what many had expected to be. The demographic distribution of votes of the generation that actually experienced Park's authoritarian reign voting overwhelmingly for Park supports this conclusion. Actual tangible outcome of effective governance won over the virtue-led challenges of its legitimacy.

Shaping by Dissatisfaction

The liberal interpretation of Rhee and Park can be summarized as historical nihilism. It takes on the form of negating the advancements throughout history and denying the meaningful aspects of it, believing that it lacks any compliance with actual virtue. Indeed, liberals have defined modern Korean history as a history of wrongness and defeat of justice. Seok Heon Hahm puts it as "a beggar of suffering" and writes with pity "A queen of suffering is trying to give birth to a new king, but has no power to do so. The cries of that pain are the Korean War, the April Revolution and the May coup. Alas, she is still going to die". While this view was greatly revised in 1965 through his second edition, this defeatist sentiment perpetuates the writing of modern leftist intellectuals.

The roots of this defeatist perception can be explained through liberal doctrines and how these doctrines impact the political sphere. As discussed earlier, liberals are pursuers of ideal social virtues such as freedom and equality. Their set objective is constructing a society where these virtues are fulfilled. Moreover, as they perceive the existence of two conflicting worlds, they tend to antagonize the other world of status quo that is not and even an obstacle against the construction of utopia. This tendency has resulted in Korean liberals approaching domestic politics with dichotomy. A major arguable flaw with this approach is that this dichotomy is a simplistic "good v. evil" mindset encompasses the liberal faction's own discontent about how Korea has progressed since 1945. Two principal dichotomies are "Nation (both as an individual and a group)" and "People". Another is more commonplace: "the privileged minority" and "the unprivileged majority".

The first interpretive dichotomy, the nation versus the people, has been always prevalent and allows liberals to differentiate the public that the regime sees as a mobilization force and civil society. While analyzing the speeches of the 2012 Presidential candidates, analysts found that liberal candidate Jaein Moon tended to use the term "citizen" or "nation" and "people" separately. Moon held a negative connotation on the former. It could be concluded that Moon created a contrast of "ignorant nation" against "liberally enlightened people" (E. Park). This is an example of how liberals perceive themselves as intellectually and morally superior based on their doctrines, what conservatives criticize as "intellectual haughtiness" under the critique of theory (Muller). This dichotomy influences historical interpretation as liberals do not consider the nation and the people to be a single entity. Liberals see numerous occasions when the state tried to draw the mass into nationhood by forceful fascist means, which they believe that the mass has no genuine or voluntary connection to. Liberals, who are anti-state, are both skeptical of and resentful toward Rhee and Park.

The second dichotomy, the privileged minority versus the unprivileged majority, can also be identified through liberal figures. Former President Muhyeon Roh stated in 2003 that "Justice was vanquished in this country by the ones with vested interests" and President Yeongsam Kim stated in 1993, shockingly as he is considered as one of the more conservative democratic leaders, "Now it will be a period where the ones who have will suffer" (Cho). The liberal emphasis on equality has led them to label private institutions and beneficiaries that have grown under the aid of the government, as foes of democracy and moral values. When a volume of criticisms against Samsung is becoming a bestseller, it is easy to see that such hostility aimed at "the privileged" is dominating the mind of many, particularly youths who view the Chaebeols as reactionary forces (Cho). While liberal historical interpretation in Korea is, not that different from liberal judgments in other countries that emphasize from equality and equity, Korean liberals' class consciousness overwhelms the fact that Korea's establishment and growth was directed by Rhee, Park and their institutions and leads liberals to concentrate on the poorly compensated sacrifice of the proletariat.

Liberals' historical perception emphasizes opposition against conservative institutions and is founded on their trademark of prioritizing values as ends versus means. They use this negative sentiment to rally public opinion, a strategy typical as seen in the 2012 Presidential election. Conservative Geunhye Park's legitimacy as future President was questioned. Liberals asked whether the daughter of a dictator can materialize the modern demands of a democracy. While liberal strategy failed to prevent Park from getting elected, liberals still pride themselves and concentrate on assuring the public that they are "the only group that can start a reformative wave" (N. Lee).

Conclusion

Modern Korean history, with its disconnection between its pre-modern era and its modern era, is vulnerable to an ideology-based clash over interpretation. The conservative view on how societal issues should be handled and executed, informed by the four conservative pillars, has led conservatives to positively evaluate the influence of Rhee and Park's Presidencies and venerate their contribution to nation-building. The liberal view is critical of Rhee and Park's suppression of democratic values and their perceived negative effects on current Korean society. The ongoing debate about this different evaluation exemplifies why this interpretive difference is important, impacting the two factions' stance and affecting their legitimacy. Korean politics is serving as a historical battlefield where both sides are brandishing their version of Rhee and Park with a political purpose.

WORKS CITED

Bailyn, Bernard. *The Debate on the Constitution: Federalist and Anti-federalist Speeches, Articles, and Letters During the Struggle over Ratification.* New York: Library of America, 1993. Print.

Burke, Edmund. *Reflections on the Revolution in France.* New York: Oxford University Press, 2009. Print.

Burke, Edmund. *Thoughts and Details on Scarcity.* Whitefish: Kessinger Publishing, 2005. Print.

Cho, Woo Seok. *I'm Conservative.* Seoul: East Asia, 2011. Print.

Choi, Hong Yeol. "Collapse of the Nation by Making Cafeteria Free" *chosun.com* Chosun

Daily, 6 Dec. 2012. Web. 14 May. 2013.

Choi, Jang Jip. *Democracy After Democratization.* Seoul: Humanitas, 2002. Print.

Cummings, Bruce. *Korea's Place in the Sun.* New York: W.W. Norton & Company, 1997. Print.

Cummings, Bruce. *The Korean War.* New York: The Modern Library, 2010. Print.

Durant, Will. *The Story of Philosophy: The Lives and Opinions of the World's Great Philosophers.* New York: Pocket Books, 1991. Print.

Greene, Abigail. *Fatherlands: State-Building and Nationhood in Nineteenth-Century Germany.* New York: Cambridge University Press, 2001. Print.

Hahm, Seok Heon. *Korean History Seen in Meaning.* Seoul: Hangilsa, 2006. Print.

Henderson, Gregory. *Korea: The Politics of the Vortex.* Cambridge: Harvard University Press, 1968. Print.

Kim, Jae Hong. *Park Chung Hee Gene.* Seoul: Gaemagowon, 2012. Print.

Kropotkin, Peter Alexeyevich. *Mutual Aid: A Factor of Evolution.* Charleston: Forgotten Books, 2008. Print.

Kwon, Taejun. *Korea Jumping over a Century.* Seoul: Nannam Publisher, 2006. Print.

Lee, Kyeong Ho. "UPP elects Lee and Shim: 'I am the rightful liberal" *asiae.co.kr* Asia Economics, 21 Oct. 2012. Web. 20 Jan. 2013.

Lee, Nami. *Korea's Conservatism and Reactionary.* Seoul: Jiseongsa, 2011. Print.

Mill, John Stuart. *On Liberty.* New York: Dover Publications, 2002. Print.

Muller Z., Jerry. *Conservatism: An anthology of social and political thought from David Hume to the present.* Princeton: Princeton University Press, 1997. Print.

Nisbet, Robert. *Conservatism: Dream and Reality.* Piscataway: Transaction Publishers, 2001. Print.

Park, Eun Ju. "Small Changes Unbearable to Conservatives" *chosun.com* Chosun Daily, 12 Jul. 2012. Web. 24 Jun. 2013.

Park, Jihyang. "Different August, Different Path"

chosun.com Chosun Daily, 16 Aug. 2012. Web. 01 Jul. 2013.

Quinton, Anthony. *Politics of Imperfection.* New York: Faber and Faber, 1978. Print.

Schuman, Michael. *The Miracle: The Epic Story of Asia's Quest for Wealth.* New York: HarperCollins, 2009. Print.

Schumpeter, Joseph. *Capitalism, Socialism and Democracy.* New York: Kessinger Publishing, 2010. Print.

Scruton, Roger. *The Meaning of Conservatism.* South Bend, Indiana: St. Augustine's Press, 2002. Print.

Sen, Amartya. *Poverty and Famines: An Essay on Entitlement and Deprivation.* Oxford: Clarendon Press, 1981. Print.

Song, Chang Dal. *Why Park Chung Hee is a Great President.* Seoul: GreenVision Korea, 2012. Print.

Viereck, Peter. *Conservatism: From John Adams to Churchill.* New York: Transaction Publishers, 2005. Print.

Yang, Seung Tae. "Methodological Approach to the Studies of Korean Conservatism." *Korean Political Society* 28. 2 (1994). Print.

Yang, Won Bo. "Lee Seok Gi refuses Aeguka" *joongang.com* Joongang Daily, 26 May. 2012. Web. 18 Apr. 2013.

Yoo, Yeong Ik. *Founding Father: Syngman Rhee.* Seoul: Illjogak, 2013. Print.

ABOUT THE AUTHOR

Seong Jun Park is currently a student at the University of Virginia, Charlottesville. He graduated from Bugil Academy Global Leader Program in 2014.

Born in Changwon, Gyeongnam Province, Korea, he is the grandson of two Korean War veterans who drove him to have particular interests in modern Korean history.

www.ingramcontent.com/pod-product-compliance
Lightning Source LLC
Chambersburg PA
CBHW070811290526
45795CB00002B/682